The CanniBal AnaconDa

by G.C. McRae

Illustrations by David Anderson

A Bunky Mutt Book

For Nora

BUNKY MUTT BOOKS
Published by MacDonald Warne Media

Copyright © G.C.McRae 2011
All Rights Reserved

Illustrations by David Anderson

Cover and Interior Design by Dianna Little

ISBN 978-0-9876845-0-9

Bunky Mutt is a trademark of MacDonald Warne Media

Cannibal Anaconda is produced only in eco-friendly POD and eBook editions.

Visit us at:

www.bunkymutt.com
www.gcmcrae.com
www.davidandersonillustration.com

One rainy day my mother went
to the fridge to find some cheese
I'd asked her for a little snack
Saying, mother, may I, please

But when she opened up
the door of the fridge
the cheese was totally gone
Not a crumb was left in the package
Something was terribly wrong

She came round the corner
And told me not to lie
She wanted to know who did it
And while she looked me in the eye
I said,

It was the cannibal anaconda
and his band of mutineers
with their gribby grabby hands
and their ten foot spears
I swear they made me do it
I didn't stand a chance
They tied me to the fridge
and put me in a trance

My mother heaved a sigh
and her eyes began to roll
For telling me a lie, she said
Go clean the toilet bowl

The very next day my mother
decided she was going to bake
She had company coming to visit
And was gonna make chocolate cake

But when she opened up
the cupboard door
all the chocolate was gone
Not a lick was left inside the box
Something was terribly wrong
She came round the corner
And told me not to lie
She wanted to know who did it
And while she looked me in the eye
I said..

It was the cannibal anaconda
and his band of mutineers
with their gribby grabby hands
and their ten foot spears
I swear they made me do it
I didn't stand a chance
They tied me to the fridge
and put me in a trance

My mother heaved a sigh
and her eyes began to bug
For telling me a lie, she said
Go vacuum up the rug

The very next day my mother
Was gonna give us all some chips
She had the bowl all ready
And a little garlic dip
But when she opened up
the pantry door
all the chips were gone
Not a speck of salt was left in the bag
Something was terribly wrong

She came round the corner
And told me not to lie
She wanted to know who did it
And while she looked me in the eye
I said..

15

It was the cannibal anaconda
and his band of mutineers
with their gribby grabby hands
and their ten foot spears
I swear they made me do it
I didn't stand a chance
They tied me to the fridge
and put me in a trance

My mother heaved a sigh
I swear she nearly swore
For telling me a lie, she said
Go wash the kitchen floor

The very next day my mother
Was gonna make some peanut brittle
We always loved to eat it up
Ever since we were little
But when she opened up
the cupboard door
all the peanut butter was gone
Not a glop was left inside the jar
Something was terribly wrong

She came round the corner
And told me not to lie
She wanted to know who did it
And while she looked me in the eye
I said..

It was the cannibal anaconda
and his band of mutineers
with their gribby grabby hands
and their ten foot spears
I swear they made me do it
I didn't stand a chance
They tied me to the fridge
and put me in a trance

My mother heaved a sigh
She just stared and couldn't blink
For telling me a lie, she said
Go scrub the bathroom sink

Then one rainy day my mother
Was gonna make a cherry pie
She always kept the can of filling
In the closet really high
But when she opened up
the closet door
all the cherry filling was gone
I heard her scream and ran to see
Something was terribly wrong

She came running round the corner
And said it was no lie
Now she knew who did it
And while I looked her in the eye
She said..

It's the cannibal anaconda
and a band of mutineers
with their gribby grabby hands
and their ten foot spears
I swear they're in the closet
We don't stand a chance
They're gonna tie us to the fridge
and put us in a trance

I folded up my arms
I heaved a great big sigh
Mother dear, I said to her
You should never tell a lie

CPSIA information can be obtained
at www.ICGtesting.com
Printed in the USA
LVIC06n1310300913
354697LV00003B